Zigzag

The Sound of Z

By Alice K. Flanagan

Zip! A zipper goes zigzag when it is zipped.

Zap! Lightning goes zigzag when it zaps.

5

A snake goes zigzag when it moves.

What goes zigzag to you?

10

This wall goes zigzag up a hill.

This road goes zigzag down a hill.

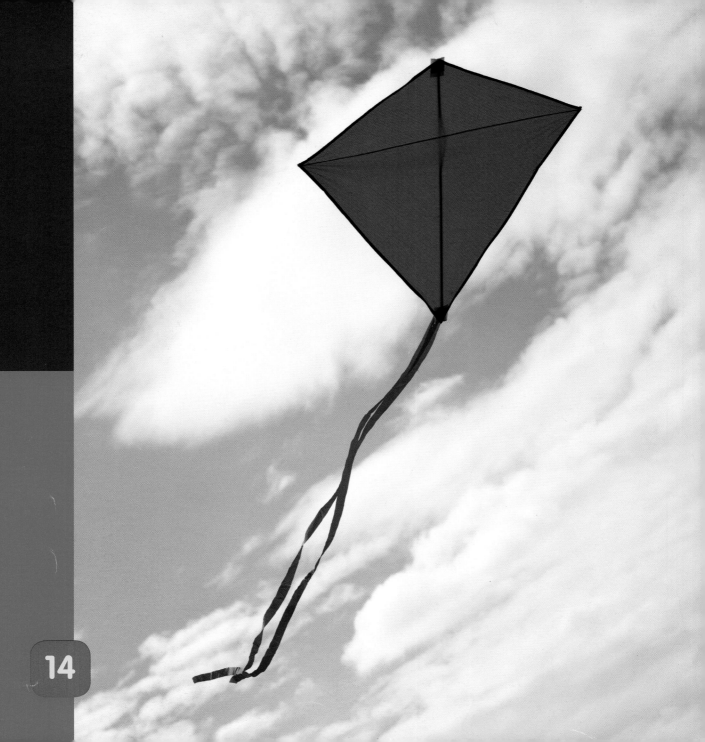

14

A kite goes zigzag in the wind.

Some things cut zigzag for you.

18

This arrow goes zigzag on a sign.

Z goes zigzag all the time.

21

Word List:

zap

zaps

zigzag

zip

zipped

zipper

Note to Parents and Educators

The books in this series are based on current research, which supports the idea that our brains are pattern-detectors rather than rules-appliers. This means children learn to read easier when they are taught the familiar spelling patterns found in English. As children encounter more complex words, they have greater success in figuring out these words by using the spelling patterns.

Throughout the series, the texts provide the reader with the opportunity to practice and apply knowledge of the sounds in natural language. The books introduce sounds using familiar onsets and *rimes*, or spelling patterns, for reinforcement.

For example, the word *cat* might be used to present the short "a" sound, with the letter *c* being the onset and "_at" being the rime. This approach provides practice and reinforcement of the short "a" sound, as there are many familiar words made with the "_at" rime.

The stories and accompanying photographs in this series are based on time-honored concepts in children's literature: well-written, engaging texts and colorful, high-quality photographs combine to produce books that children want to read again and again.

Dr. Peg Ballard
Minnesota State University, Mankato

23

The Child's World®
childsworld.com

Published by The Child's World®
1980 Lookout Drive • Mankato, MN 56003-1705
800-599-READ • www.childsworld.com

ACKNOWLEDGMENTS
The Child's World®: Mary Swensen, Publishing Director
The Design Lab: Design
Michael Miller: Editing

PHOTO CREDITS
© Chokniti Khongchum/Shutterstock.com: 13; Daniel
Prudek/Shutterstock.com: 10; Drozhzhina Elena/
Shutterstock.com: cover; everydayplus/Shutterstock.com:
2; Everything/Shutterstock.com: 17; Johan Swanepoel/
Shutterstock.com: 5; Lex-art/Shutterstock.com: 21; Michael
Dechev/Shutterstock.com: 14; Michiel de Wit/Shutterstock.
com: 6; Pavel L Photo and Video/Shutterstock.com: 9;
Sopotnicki/Shutterstock.com: 18

ISBN 9781503809277
LCCN 2015958493

Printed in the United States of America
Mankato, MN
June, 2016
PA02310

ABOUT THE AUTHOR

Alice K. Flanagan lives with her husband in Chicago, Illinois, and writes books for children and teachers. Ever since she was a young girl, Ms. Flanagan has enjoyed writing. Today, she has more than 70 books published on a wide variety of topics. Some of the books she has written include biographies of U.S. presidents and first ladies; biographies of people working in our neighborhoods; phonics books for beginning readers; informational books about birds; and career education in the classroom.